Little Wild Chimpanzee

A READ ALONE BOOK

by Anna Michel

pictures by
Peter and Virginia Parnall

PANTHEON BOOKS

Published in the United States by Pantheon Books,
a division of Random House, Inc., New York, and simultaneously
in Canada by Random House of Canada Limited, Toronto.
Manufactured in the United States of America
10 9 8 7 6 5 4 3 2 1 0
Library of Congress Cataloging in Publication Data
Michel, Anna. Little wild chimpanzee. (A Read alone book)
Summary: Follows the growth, development, and
training of Little Chimp until at age five he has his first solo
experience.   1. Chimpanzees—Juvenile literature.
2. Animals, Infancy of—Juvenile literature.   [1. Chimpanzees.
2. Animals—Infancy]   I. Parnall, Virginia.   II. Parnall, Peter.
III. Title. QL737.P96M53 599′.884 77-20986 QL737.P96M53 599′.844
77-20986 ISBN 0-394-83560-3 ISBN 0-394-93560-8 lib.bdg.

for Betty Miles

Little Chimp was born

in the rain forest of Africa,

where the wild chimpanzees live.

"Waa-hoo! Waa-hoo! Waa-hoo!"

All the chimpanzees screamed

when Little Chimp was born.

They crowded around to get

a close look at

the new chimpanzee.

Little Chimp did not mind.

He held tight to Mother Chimp's hair

and stared back at them

with enormous eyes.

Sister Chimp was very curious.

All day long she watched Little Chimp.

He was tiny, and wrinkled, and almost bald.

Sister Chimp wanted to know more

about her new brother.

But every time she tried to touch him,

Mother Chimp pushed her hand away.
So Sister Chimp found a long stick
and touched Little Chimp with it.
Then she sniffed the end of the stick.
The stick was a tool to help her find out
what a baby chimpanzee smells like.

Every day Mother Chimp and Sister Chimp

walked many miles looking for food.

A three-month-old chimp cannot walk.

So Little Chimp rode along, upside down,

hanging from Mother Chimp's hairy tummy.

Sister Chimp was six years old.

She ate fruit and leaves and insects,

just like Mother Chimp.

Little Chimp was too young

to eat these things.

He drank Mother Chimp's milk instead.

When Little Chimp was five months old,
he rode in a new way.
Mother Chimp placed him on her back.
At first he slipped down many times.
But Mother Chimp always caught him
and put him back again.
With practice, he became a good rider.

One day Little Chimp let go of his mother

for the first time in his whole life.

He took his first step—

and fell on his ear!

Little Chimp tried and tried again.

Each day his wobbly legs took him

a little farther from Mother Chimp.

Little Chimp learned to climb, too.

Climbing up was easy.

Climbing down was hard.

Mother Chimp or Sister Chimp

always came to help.

13

Every night when the sun set,

Little Chimp watched Mother Chimp

build a nest out of branches and leaves.

She always chose a safe spot,

high in a treetop.

Sister Chimp built her own nest nearby.

Little Chimp slept with Mother Chimp

in her treetop nest

until the sun came up again.

Even when he was one year old,

Little Chimp still slept with his mother.

But now he tried to build nests

just the way Mother Chimp did.

First he bent back branches.

Then he piled leaves onto the branches.

When one nest was finished,

he jumped up and down on it

until it fell apart.

Then he built another nest.

When that one was finished,

he jumped on it until it fell apart, too.

Little Chimp kept on building nests

and breaking them, again and again.

16

Once Little Chimp built a nest
very high up in a tree.
He jumped on this nest, too.
But this time Little Chimp fell.
He grabbed onto a very thin branch,
and he screamed as loud as he could.
Mother Chimp climbed up the tree
and carried Little Chimp to safety.

If other chimps and baboons were around,

Little Chimp and Sister Chimp

had friends to play with.

They chased and climbed

and danced together.

Sometimes they made so much noise

they bothered the grown-up chimps.

One time Mother Chimp wanted to leave.

But Little Chimp was having

too much fun with his friends.

Mother Chimp tried to pull him away.

But again and again he ran back to play.

Then Mother Chimp grabbed

Little Chimp's foot.

Little Chimp laughed as she

dragged him behind her.

Thump! Thump! Thump!

He thought it was a game.

Little Chimp liked to watch while

Sister Chimp gathered food.

She poked a stick into an ants' nest.

When she pulled the stick out,

it was covered with ants.

Sister Chimp licked the ants off

and poked the stick back in for more.

Then Little Chimp

jumped on Sister Chimp's back

and knocked the stick out of her hand.

Sister Chimp pushed him away.

Now that she was older,

she did not always want to play.

She wanted to gather food.

Soon Little Chimp tried

to catch insects, too.

He had to choose a twig

or a blade of grass

that was long enough

to reach the insects in their nests.

He had to pull the twig out

very slowly and carefully,

so he would not lose the insects.

Learning this took a long time.

One day Little Chimp wanted to play.

But Mother Chimp and Sister Chimp

would not play with him.

Just then Little Chimp heard something.

He sat very still and listened.

It was the sound of baboons.

But where were they?

Little Chimp climbed a tree.

He looked off in every direction.

Then he rushed down the tree and

ran off to find the baboons.

When Mother Chimp turned around,

Little Chimp was gone.

Mother Chimp climbed a tree.

She looked and looked.

No Little Chimp!

She listened and listened.

No Little Chimp!

All she heard were the sounds

of a baboon troop.

Mother Chimp grew very nervous.

She called out to Sister Chimp.

But when they left to find Little Chimp,

they went in the wrong direction!

Little Chimp and Little Baboon
were old friends.
When they saw each other,
they began to play.
They wrestled, and tickled,
and chased each other through the trees.
They played for hours and hours.
When the sun began to go down,
Little Chimp and his friend
looked all around.
No Mother Baboon!
No Mother Chimp!
They hurried through the forest
looking for their mothers.
Soon it was dark.

Even though he was
frightened and tired,
Little Chimp knew what to do.
He climbed a tree
and built a sleeping nest.
This was the first time Little Chimp
had slept without his mother.
And Little Baboon had always slept
sitting on a tree limb
next to Mother Baboon.
When he saw Little Chimp's cozy nest,
he climbed up, too.
Little Baboon felt safer
sitting near Little Chimp's nest.

In the morning
Little Chimp and Little Baboon
climbed down from the tree.
They were hungry.
When they came to an ants' nest,
Little Chimp broke off a twig
and trimmed the leaves.
He stuck the twig into the nest
and carefully pulled it out again.
It was covered with juicy, red ants.
Little Chimp licked them off.
Then Little Chimp gave the twig
to his friend.
But baboons do not use tools.
Little Baboon just looked at the twig.
Then he threw it away.

31

Suddenly they heard a baboon bark.

Little Baboon barked back.

It was Mother Baboon.

She had found her baby.

For a while Little Chimp

followed the baboon troop

through the forest.

But then he saw something

that made him stop.

It was a tree full of ripe, red palm nuts.

Little Chimp grunted.

His hair stood on end.

Then he climbed right up the tree

and began to eat.

Little Chimp ate one palm nut—
two palm nuts—three palm nuts—
and he kept right on eating!
Then he smelled something.
The smell was so strong
that it made him stop eating.

Little Chimp looked down.

What he saw made him

scream out in fright.

It was a leopard!

Little Chimp climbed up higher to get away.

But the leopard began to climb up, too.

Just then Little Chimp heard something.

"Wraaaa!"

Chimpanzees were coming!

They screamed and threw rocks
at the leopard.

Then the leopard was gone.

The chimpanzees had frightened
him away.

Little Chimp hurried down the tree
to greet his mother and sister.
Mother Chimp kissed her son many times.
Sister Chimp tickled his chin.
Then they went to eat palm nuts
with the other chimpanzees.
It had been a big adventure for Little Chimp.
And now he was back with his family.

In a few years
Little Chimp will be grown.
Then he will take care of himself.
He will venture out alone
or with other male chimpanzees.
He will hunt for his own food,
sleep in his own nest at night,
and be a father.
Even when Little Chimp is grown,
he will not forget Mother Chimp
or Sister Chimp,
and he will often visit them.

But then Little Chimp
will no longer be little.
Then he will be Big Chimp.

ABOUT THE AUTHOR

Anna Michel received her M.S. degree from
Bank Street College and has been a teacher and a
reading specialist. Her fascination with chimpanzees
led to her working with the chimp subject of a
language acquisition research project at Columbia
University and to her writing *Little Wild Chimpanzee*.
She is married and lives in New York City.

ABOUT THE ARTISTS

Peter and Virginia Parnall live with their son and
daughter on a coastal Maine farm. Mr. Parnall has
illustrated over fifty books for children and is
well known for his beautiful drawings. Virginia
Parnall has worked with her husband on a number
of his books.